I

THE FIRST FACTORY ACTS

The factory acts were the first attempt at state control of the exploitation of the labouring classes since the failure of the early Stuarts. Their success was therefore vital to the development of modern social administration.

Control was needed because of the application of power to machinery, which, in the last two decades of the eighteenth century began to move first spinning and later weaving from parlours and worksheds into factories. In 1795 a group of doctors at Manchester who had formed a board of health to investigate a local outbreak of putrid fever gave the alarm. They pointed out that children herded into factories formed a seedbed for infectious diseases; that their strength was impaired by long hours of day and night work; that their education and morals were neglected; and that parliament needed to establish wise and humane laws for the regulation of the places where they worked. Thus a precedent for the demand for public intervention to protect and educate factory children was established.

At this early period, many spinning mills, operated by water power, were tucked away in Pennine valleys or by Midland mill ponds. Since child labour was needed, and was not available locally, millowners were compelled to import the neglected, sickly and ungovernable children from London workhouses, and board them at the mills. Then evils arose from children being entirely in the power of strangers who exploited them for profit in an intensely competitive industry. Sir Robert Peel the elder, who had made a fortune with the help of child labour in his Tamworth cotton spinning mill, induced parliament in 1802 to pass the *Health and Morals of Apprentices Act*. This act confined the labour of young apprentices in textile mills to twelve hours a day, forbade them to be worked at night, laid down that they should be provided with two suits of clothes every year, that they should have proper beds (with no more than two to each) in separate sleeping quarters for males and females, and that they should have some elementary schooling and religious instruction. By way of health precautions, factories were to be periodically limewashed, and infectious diseases medically attended and reported. The act was an attempt to enforce on all employers the reasonable conditions provided by the most humane millowners for their factory apprentices.

When Peel tried again in 1815 circumstances had altered. As steam gradually replaced water power, more mills were built near coalfields. Some wealthy and paternal millowners planned factory communities, while round other factories speculative builders ran up two-roomed shacks or back-to-back dwellings. Children were now brought to work by their parents, and masters accepted less responsibility for them. Nearly all early industries used child assistants. In Glasgow spinning mills in the 1830's, one male spinner might work with a little piecer (or piecener), an outside piecer, and an inside piecer, ranging in age from 9, to 13 or 14 and over, and progressing in wages from about 2s. 6d. a week to about 6s. 3d. He engaged and paid them out of his own wages of £2, and usually employed his own children. The little piecers had to creep under machines six inches above the floor, and their small fingers were especially useful in fine spinning, to tie broken ends. Children worked alongside adults throughout a working day which was normally twelve hours, but, in a rush of orders, might be far longer. It has been suggested that stories of cruelty to factory children have been deliberately exaggerated. However that may be, operatives carried conviction when they testified that they had to thrash their piecers to keep them awake towards the end of the day. The group worked as a team, so that the restriction of children's hours could dislocate production. One of the most demoralising features of the system was the small proportion of trained adult spinners to children and young women, which spelled dead-end jobs. Parents became dependent on the labour of their infants. If the father was a handloom weaver, entangled in a decaying trade with wages gradually sinking to starvation level, he might have to hire out his children to a strange spinner. These spinners sometimes paid their piecers wages in inverse proportion to the kindness and consideration with which they treated them, and the children, hired to the highest bidder, would be at his mercy in the mill. Inducement to hire out children was to increase in the 1830's, when the coupling of mules (spindle carriages), and then the introduction of self-acting mules put many adult spinners out of work.

Peel's new bill was largely based on the suggestions of Robert Owen, manager of the famous New Lanark factory with its model village and model schools, and it was backed by a parliamentary select committee. But by now the millowners had organised their opposition. The bill was delayed, referred to a select committee of the Lords, and emasculated. The act which eventually passed in 1819, applied only to cotton mills. It laid down a minimum age of nine for the employment of children, and restricted the hours of work for those under sixteen to 12 a day between 5 a.m. and 9 p.m. with $1\frac{1}{2}$ off for meals. This, however, was weakened by provisions for extra work hours when water mills had lost time through breakdown or drought.

Peel's efforts were continued by the radical M.P., Sir John Cam Hobhouse. But his acts of 1825 and 1831 were as unsuccessful as the earlier ones. No way had been found of enforcing any of them. The act of 1802 had provided for visits of inspection by local magistrates and clergy. But many magistrates were millowners, and neither they nor their clerical neighbours would enforce regulations conflicting with their own interests and local opinion. The act of 1819 had relied on rewards to informers. But although the jealousies of competing manufacturers were always a help both in securing legislation and in preventing one factory from undercutting its neighbours by working illegal hours, only the workers in the factories really knew what went on inside them, and they were too scared of their masters to inform on them. Hobhouse's device of age certificates from parents for factory children was, as will be seen, equally unreliable. It was soon said that the act of 1831 was universally ignored.

This failure to observe the laws, and with it the whole question of excessive working hours, especially as they affected children and young women, became increasingly serious as the factory population grew. It has been calculated that by 1835 there were some 1000 cotton mills operating in England, with another 135 in Scotland and 29 in Ireland; and this leaves out of consideration the woollen and worsted mills of Yorkshire, the linen factories of Belfast and Glasgow, the silk of Macclesfield, and other textile industries. Edward Baines in his *History of the Cotton Manufacture* reckons that at least 237,000 people were employed in the cotton mills. According to the *Victoria County History for Lancashire* there were 218,000 cotton mill hands in that county alone, of whom 13.2% were children under thirteen and nearly half were women from thirteen upwards. This was the largest single group of workers in a total manufacturing population reckoned in the 1831 census at about 3,000,000 in a nation of approximately 24,000,000. The protection of textile workers had become by this time a large-scale problem, although not so enormous as to make it impossible to handle, always provided some administrative machinery could be devised to do it.

II

THE SHORT TIME MOVEMENT

After 1830 the struggle for factory legislation was transformed by the rise of the Short Time movement in the industrial districts. The idea of compulsory curtailment of the working day for children and young persons to ten hours had been mooted back in 1825 by a trio of Yorkshire spinning masters, but its most colourful exponent was to be Richard Oastler, an unsuccessful Leeds merchant who had succeeded his father as resident steward to an absentee country squire, Thornhill of Fixby Hall. Oastler really started the movement in Yorkshire with his demand that the legislative protection at least nominally afforded to children in cotton mills should be extended to those in woollen mills too. His opening letter of 29th September 1830 to the *Leeds Mercury*, entitled "Slavery in Yorkshire", was couched in the romantic rhetoric fashionable at the time.

"The very streets which received the droppings of an 'Anti Slavery Society'," wrote Oastler (getting at the Whig industrialists who supported slave emancipation in the West Indies), "are every morning wet by the tears of innocent victims at the accursed shrine of avarice, who are *compelled* (not by the cartwhip of the negro slave-driver but by the dread of the equally appalling thong or strap of the overlooker), to hasten, half dressed *but not half fed*, to those magazines of infantile slavery—*the worsted mills in the town and neighbourhood of Bradford!!!*" He asked why children in worsted mills should not be protected by legislative enactments as well as those who worked in cotton mills, and urged that christians should feel and act for those whom Christ so eminently loved and declared that 'of such is the Kingdom of Heaven.'[1]

Accordingly, in the spring of 1831, committees of workmen to support Hobhouse's bill were founded in the Yorkshire woollen towns. Oastler, who had been persuaded to ally with the Huddersfield Committee, and was now demanding a ten-hour day, wrote letter after letter to the *Leeds Mercury* until its whig editor, Edward Baines, refused to publish them, and he fell back on its tory rival, the *Leeds Intelligencer*. He was supported by a crowd of pamphleteers and rhymers, whose poetic intentions were, alas, not always realised in their performance.

> "And like a slave, her feeble helpless pow'rs
> Are doom'd to work at least for thirteen hours"

sang the author of *The Factory Child*.

Lancashire gave the movement a new twist by demanding restrictions of the hours of operation of the machinery itself, which would be easier to check than the working hours of different classes of labourers. Glasgow, too, soon had its Short Time committees.

The Short Time movement rapidly became entangled in politics. Along with the Anti-Slavery movement upon whose whig supporters the Short Timers continued to heap contumely for their concern with black slavery while they practised white child slavery, it campaigned throughout the struggles for the 1832 reform bill. In 1837 Oastler led the committees into battle against the new poor law. Many of them were, in fact, also trade union branches. Their members became chartists or were attracted to Owenite socialism, and here they parted company with the tories among their leaders. The Short Time movement has to be seen as one aspect of the working class awakening of the 1830's and 1840's.

---

[1] A letter in support of Hobhouse's second bill in 1831 is an even better example of Oaster's hyperbolic strain:

"The Harps which your little ones had prepared to attune in grateful strains to the songs of liberty, must now be hung upon the willows . . . Bend not however to despair—but trust in God and in yourselves.—The God of Justice, of Mercy, and of Truth, still reigns—If they still resist and steel themselves against His laws, in anger He will speak and make the oppressors quake!"

He told the operatives to exact from parliamentary candidates a pledge to support "Ten hours a day and a time-book bill."

Among the most influential supporters of the movement were a number of philanthropic millowners who, like the elder Peel, wanted to protect children from excessive labour and needed legislative protection against less scrupulous competitors. The Lancashire cotton masters John Fielden (zealous campaigner for an eight hour day), Joseph Brotherton and Charles Hindley, along with the Leeds merchant M. T. Sadler and later the aristocrat Lord Ashley (after 1851, earl of Shaftesbury), formed the movement's parliamentary group. Radical working men, some Anglican clergymen, and the occasional landowner formed its local leaders and its rank and file. The philanthropic factory owners included every denomination from methodist to unitarian. The tory demagogue Joseph Rayner Stephens was an independent minister expelled from the Methodist Conference. However, many prominent leaders, including the wealthy Bradford worsted spinner, John Wood, who brought Oastler into the movement, Oastler himself, parson George Stringer Bull, Sadler and Shaftesbury, adhered to the evangelical wing of the Church of England, professing a form of christian faith which may have helped to fortify them against the fashionable belief in Political Economy.[1] Since it was impossible in the nineteenth century to keep religion out of politics and many factory owners were nonconformist, the movement's propaganda, especially in the unbridled mouth of Oastler, sometimes took on an unfortunate tinge of anti-dissenting intolerance.[2]

In 1832 Oastler succeeded in organising a tory-radical electoral alliance at Halifax and Leeds against the whig millowners, their candidate the historian T. B. Macaulay, and their apologist Edward Baines of the *Leeds Mercury*. Many socially-concerned tories looked backward to a pre-industrial neo-feudal golden age.

---

[1] 'Political Economy', a contemporary term which covers laissez-faire ideas on society and economics.

[2] Witness his attack in 1835 on a master who had been fined for working a child thirteen hours without a break:

"Yes, Mr Baines, this Master Joseph Schofield must be a *very* "pious", "respectable", "humane", "charitable" man. He is quite a "pillar" in the dissenting "church" . . . "Satan is pleased such Saintship to behold" and so, Baines, are you. Your Dissenters may call such as these "saints", "pillars" and "deacons", but as long as I have pen or tongue to use I will denounce them as *the Cardinal Legates from the Court of Hell!*"

At the other extreme socialists, mostly at this time communitarians, looked forward to a golden age in which society should be so organised that the workman kept the value his labour had created; while working-class radicals simply believed that universal suffrage would enable them to make parliament attend to all their needs. The intervention of Owenite socialists could endanger the unity of the movement, but the political differences of tory and radical did not prevent them combining against the effects of classical Political Economy and social laissez-faire which constituted the gospel of cotton kings and the factory lobby. This alliance of tory gentry with working-class radicals against industrial middle-class liberalism was described in the early novels and political writings of Benjamin Disraeli, although that politician's practical support of factory control and other working-class causes was half-hearted. At the centre of politics working-class sympathisers were always at a disadvantage. The tory party was split; its "conservative" wing had swallowed Political Economy whole. The social policies of Peel and Graham were indistinguishable from those of the whig Home Secretary, Russell, or President of the Board of Trade, Poulett Thomson, who were always more prone to yield to the demands of factory owners than factory workers.

III

THE TEN HOURS STRUGGLE

Disappointment with the effects of Hobhouse's act of 1831 soon produced an all-out attempt to gain a statutory ten hour day. In December of that year M. T. Sadler introduced a bill restricting the working day of all textile workers between nine (the minimum age) and eighteen, to ten hours. He proposed to enforce it by making managers keep time books which could be inspected by the magistrates, and by age certificates with heavy penalties for fraud. M. W. Thomas in his book *The Early Factory Legislation* has pointed out that there was no provision in this bill for education, and no enforcement machinery which had not already failed. The restriction of hours for all up to eighteen was intended to close the factories after ten hours. The owners maintained that to keep expensive plant idle for 14 hours daily would render production so costly as to price them out of the foreign markets. They accused the Ten-Hour men of whipping up public concern for children in order to conceal their short-sighted attempt to restrict adult working hours, and thus, by creating an artificial scarcity of labour, to raise wages.

The whig government listened to the factory lobby, and instead of his bill Sadler got a parliamentary select committee. Before this committee a procession of operatives, medical men, and crippled children testified to the cruelties of masters and overseers and the hardships of the factory system. On a less emotional level the workmen's leaders argued that the real danger to production was not from foreign competition (which they derided) but from under-consumption at home due to poverty. Shorter hours, they said, would spread employment and keep up wages. The masters, however, insisted that shorter hours would mean lower wages, if not mass unemployment. When the session ended the committee published the evidence against the masters, who now added a rankling feeling of injustice to their dislike of government interference. They took their revenge by mobilising the new £10 householders in the first election after the reform act to run Macaulay against Sadler as M.P. for Leeds. But the defeat of Sadler did them no good. The Leeds committee sent Oastler and Bull to London to choose a new parliamentary champion; and the thirty-one year old tory evangelical Lord Ashley turned out to be a patient, persistent and formidable representative of the factory reformers.

Ashley's new Ten Hour Bill, introduced amid a flood of mass meetings, demonstrations and pilgrimages in the North, was again side-stepped, this time by the appointment of a royal commission. The furious Short Time committees refused all cooperation with the commissioners. They believed the royal commission was intended to whitewash the owners and prevent factory reform.

IV

THE ROYAL COMMISSION AND THE FACTORY ACT OF 1833

The royal commission consisted of three central commissioners helped by peripatetic local assistant commissioners armed with long questionnaires. Unlike members of a parliamentary select committee they were not M.P.s but were appointed and paid by the government. The commissioners could call for documents, examine witnesses on oath, and were not interrupted by the end of the parliamentary session. The central commissioners were Thomas Tooke, Thomas Southwood Smith, and Edwin Chadwick, all friends and disciples of the late Jeremy Bentham. Chadwick was the most unbending of Bentham's circle. How far these 'Benthamites' really followed Bentham's ideas is a complicated question. For practical purposes the group could be identified by its strong adherence to Political Economy, and economic laissez-faire, combined with its strong demand for state intervention in social matters to promote "the greatest happiness of the greatest number", or "the common interest". In the factory question the two somewhat inconsistent halves of this creed could be reconciled by insisting that adult "free" labour was outside the sphere of legislation, while children must be protected. Chadwick contrived to take a leading part in the factory commission, the poor law commission (for which he was currently taking evidence), police reform, sanitary reform and indirectly, the development of public education for which all Benthamites (along with Scottish whigs and other liberals) had a missionary zeal. As well as Chadwick's, other names from the same group appear repeatedly in the commissions of inquiry as well as in the ensuing administrative commissions, in all these fields. Most "philanthropic" in sanitation and education, their harshest side emerged in the foundation of the Victorian poor law. Their prejudices were middle class, and for all the fake hedonism of Benthamite doctrine their attitudes were frequently puritanical. They had social affinities with the industrialists, and the Short Time men had some grounds for their suspicions.

The royal commission's first report steered a course between the millowners and the factory reformers, albeit somewhat nearer the former than the latter. It discounted tales of deliberate cruelty which it said had largely died out, except in small remote factories where the workmen sometimes knocked their assistants about. But it found that the labour of children, tied to that of adults, was intolerably exhausting, debilitating, and left no time nor energy for education. It poured scorn on the economic arguments and the proposed remedies of the Short Time committees and trade union representatives. Ten hours labour was too long for children, in whose welfare and education, the commissioners maintained, the workmen were not really concerned. Their own proposal was for an eight-hour day from the age of nine to thirteen, at which age children began to retain their earnings, be independent of their parents, and become "free agents". The children could be worked in two sets (which they denied would lengthen the adults' day to sixteen hours), and should have three or four hours' education a day. Most important, in addition to the usual sanctions, they proposed a permanent body of resident inspectors, armed with extensive powers to supervise and suggest amendments to the law.

The report took the parliamentary wind out of Ashley's bill so effectively that it was defeated in the Commons by 238 votes to 93. A government bill drafted by Chadwick on the basis of the commissioners' report was introduced and put through the House by Viscount Althorp, the Chancellor of the Exchequer. As a sop to Ashley's supporters, Althorp retained the provisions of Hobhouse's Act restricting the hours of labour of young persons between thirteen and eighteen to 12, in the daytime only. This at least quieted the workmen's fears that the children's eight hour day would greatly increase adult hours, and made the measure into what was, in fact, a twelve hour act for workers in cotton, woollen and linen mills. However, the Benthamite group on the factory commission had effectively forestalled the Short Time committees' demand for a ten hour adult working day by substituting more effective provision for the protection and education of children than the Ten Hour men had proposed. Moreover, the restrictions on child labour could only be operated by a system of shifts or relays, which neither masters nor operatives believed would work. The working class leaders in particular were irreconcileably disappointed.

V

THE INSPECTORATE

Four inspectors were appointed, to supervise four great districts covering the whole British Isles. After Robert Rickards, who had to inspect almost the whole northern textile area, had died of overwork in 1836, the districts were reorganised on the

Drawn by T. Allom.

MULE S

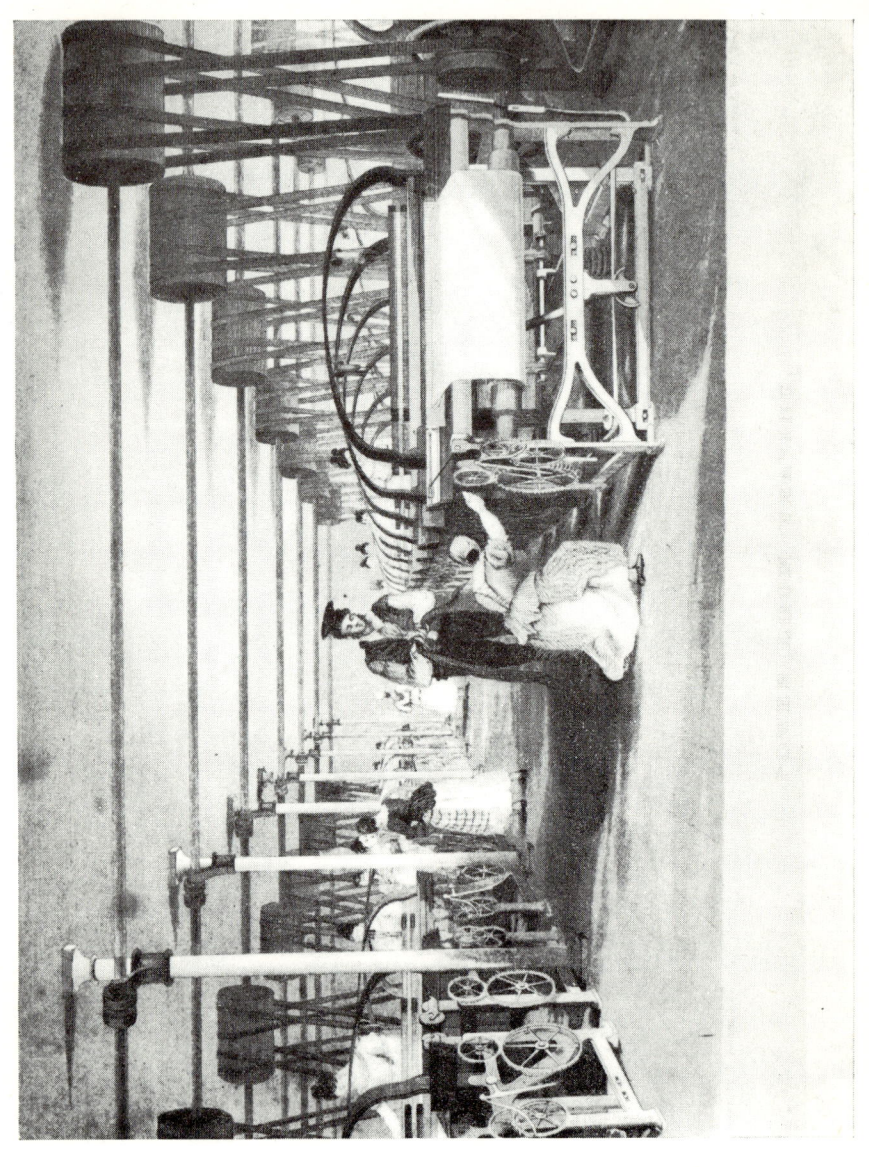

basis of a rough equality of numbers of factories. They were subdivided into two or three areas each with a resident superintendent or (after 1844) sub-inspector. The inspectors had to report quarterly or half-yearly to parliament. They were to meet periodically to coordinate their policies and issue a joint report; but until 1844 they had no central office, an inconvenience which at least muffled the outcry against "government centralisation" which pursued the Poor Law Commission. The inspectors were given a gentleman's salary of £1000 a year. This attracted educated and able men such as Leonard Horner, businessman, geologist, founder of the Edinburgh Mechanics' Institute, and first (unsuccessful) Warden of London University; T. Jones Howell, Judge Advocate of Gibraltar and Commissioner for West Indian Islands Relief, and the aggressive Scottish whig journalist, James Stuart, odd man out of the group. Horner in time established a virtual leadership over all except Stuart. Despite differences of opinion, the inspectors tended to hang together in the face of complaints from millowners to the Home Office and parliament, and petitions for their dismissal from the Short Time committees, who were watching to see that they enforced the act, and simultaneously hoping to prove it unworkable.

The superintendents received £250, later £350 a year. Until 1844 neither they nor the inspectors had additional travelling allowances, a direct incentive to stay at home and shirk the long tours of mill inspection which were their main duty. They had to keep a daily record of their work, and send weekly reports to their inspectors, a, to them, irksome practice, probably adapted from the Excise Department. All the posts in the factory service were filled by personal patronage, and some appointments (for instance that of James Stuart) were clear cases of jobbery. Perhaps for this reason several of the superintendents proved to be unsatisfactory. One was dismissed for circulating a seditious pamphlet criticising the inspectors, as well as for insolence to millowners. He had stood at Mr Parfitt's gate saying "that he was just going in here to catch a bird for his dinner tomorrow". Reappointed later at the lower rate of £250 he was finally dismissed for borrowing money from the factory masters which he could not repay. Another was an undischarged bankrupt. A third approached Lord Ashley with a list of complaints about the administration of the factory act, and having given extensive evidence before a select committee against his own inspectors, resigned. A fourth who had abetted him was sacked for supplying the tory M.P. John Fielden, with a confidential Home Office letter instructing the inspectors to report upon the state of trade and political feeling in their districts. Fielden accused the Home Secretary in the House of Commons of using the factory inspectors as spies. This superintendent was eventually reemployed and settled down. The Home Office was remarkably lenient with wrong-doers, but the civil service tradition of subordination, loyalty and political neutrality was a slow growth. The inspectors resorted to pamphlets, newspaper articles and the publication of official correspondence both to fight their critics and, on occasion, to put pressure on their political superiors. Successive Home Secretaries tried to repress these manifestations of independence, less from any theory of civil service neutrality than because of the political embarrassment they caused. Yet, as the inspectors became the recognised experts on the administration of the factory laws, their influence steadily grew, until the extension of government control over industrial conditions of employment came to depend largely on their advice.

VI

THE ENFORCEMENT OF THE FACTORY ACT

The inspectors, by policy and inclination, treated the factory owners with great politeness and circumspection. It availed them little, and enforcement soon became a war of wits between the inspectors and the millowners, who exploited every loophole in a badly worded statute. The two different lengths of working day within the same factory and work team caused great inconvenience, as masters and Short Time committees had both foreseen. Horner published schemes for relays of children which would supply assistance for adult operatives throughout a twelve hour day, but would ensure a break in the child's working hours sufficient for schooling, and even "a game of football". These were naturally distrusted by the Ten Hour men, were complicated, difficult to organise, and required more children than were available except in the great towns. In order to give the millowners time to make their arrangements, the age groups from nine to twelve were brought under the restrictions at successive six monthly intervals. In the spring of 1836, Poulett Thomson, the President of the Board of Trade, supported by the inspectors, proposed a bill to amend the act of 1833 by confining the eight hour day to children under twelve. After a stiff debate the bill passed its second reading in the House of Commons by only two votes, and the government dropped it. The masters then put up notices repudiating responsibility for those of the workmen hiring piecers who broke the law. But they still required the spinners to come with a full quota of assistants. If they did not they were dismissed. The act allowed proceedings against an operative or an overlooker who broke the law without his master's knowledge, and it was not difficult for masters to shift the penalty onto operatives or overlookers, sometimes by collusion. In Scotland, Inspector James Stuart, who was a friend of the great millowners and believed the act could not be enforced without their co-operation, refused to take any court action against the masters. Instead he persuaded them, under threat of proceedings, to dismiss any children found working illegally, and in many cases, their parents also. Although the children were often reemployed as soon as the inspector's back was turned, the gross partiality of the system became notorious.

The main difficulty in enforcing the act was not in maintaining the minimum age of nine, but in enforcing the eight hour day up to thirteen. Parents needed (or wanted) the higher wages for a full day, operatives couldn't procure enough assistants, or found paying two sets of piecers too expensive, the children detested "school", overlookers had to keep the machinery running, and masters looked the other way. Children of eleven or twelve became thirteen overnight, and the entire population of the factory districts combined to defeat the factory laws.

The paper work involved was itself a grievance. Time-books (later a register) had to be kept, showing the hours the machinery operated, and the working hours of every child and young person. Children entering the mill had to bring a certificate showing they were nine years old. They had to bring a weekly certificate signed by the teacher, showing that they had attended school for at least twelve hours in the previous week. Another age certificate was required on proceeding to the twelve hour day at thirteen. The certificates were pasted into a book which had to be kept up to date by the mill manager. They could, without legal sanction but with the inspector's encouragement, be retained to dissuade the children from changing their jobs, for medical certificates cost 6d. each.

The age certificates were subject to every kind of chicanery. Baptismal certificates often proved either to be forged or to belong to older brothers or sisters. Medical certificates were signed by local practitioners who were sometimes unqualified (the law officers of the crown refusing to lay down minimum qualifications), often under the influence of millowner patients or patrons, and sometimes intimidated by angry parents. If they gave no certificate they got no fee. Magistrates' counter-signatures were no safeguard, for the magistrates signed the certificates in batches, without seeing the children. The inspectors, by refusing to accept certificates except from doctors of their own choice, set up an unofficial system by which certificates were granted only at the mill, by a doctor appointed for each group of factories. But medical science itself had evolved no way of telling a child's age. Horner, after various enquiries about average sizes and weights, required each child proceeding to full working hours to produce a doctor's certificate that he was "of the normal strength and appearance" of thirteen. (This was an adaptation of the certificate for nine year olds starting work laid down in the 1833 act). Doctors then certified children as thirteen whom they knew to be twelve or under, and the Manchester Short Time committee petitioned for Horner's dismissal on the ground that he was trying to circumvent parliament's refusal to repeal the section of the act protecting children under thirteen. The problem was not solved until the Registrar of Births and Deaths (established in 1837 by Chadwick, partly for this very purpose), eventually supplied accurate information about children's birth dates.

Inevitably the managers had early-warning systems for the approach of inspector or superintendent. The superintendents could legally be excluded from the working part of the mill, and owners who had been offended by a prosecution kept them out. Nonetheless, children were discovered concealed in wool bags or hidden in the privies. Concealing children was not illegal; it merely created a presumption that the law was being broken. The inspectors had no power to prosecute for physical cruelty; but they could and did assist victims to prepare a case of assault for the courts.

The education provisions of the act were as troublesome to

enforce as the restrictions on working hours. To the inspectors, education, or moral training, was the main purpose of the law. Some millowners built good schools for their young workers. Many more resented the cost of providing education, which, they argued, was the responsibility of parents. Local day schools would not take children at irregular hours in filthy working clothes, but the Lords had effectively prevented good factory schools by deleting from the 1833 bill a clause to finance the construction of schoolrooms from the rates. The proceeds of fines for breaches of the act allocated to schools educating factory children were hopelessly inadequate. Too many 'schools' were housed in the coal-bunker, with a broken down operative as teacher. Even the better ones were places of detention for the children in their hours off work, and they were, on the inspectors' own admission, being cheated of their 3d. school fee.

In the last resort, inspectors depended on the magistrates to punish offenders, and so enforce the act. These, however, were the very people on whom the earlier acts had come to grief. Inevitably some magistrates seized every opportunity to dismiss charges or mitigate penalties. Fines for identical offences varied enormously between one bench of justices and another. Advantage was taken of masters' pleas of ignorance to 'mitigate' penalties to £1 or even 5s. Penalties on workmen were generally proportionately higher than on employers. Only one case could be punished at a time, and a master would pay a £1 fine for overworking a hundred children simultaneously. It was worth paying the penalty to get the work done, and the £1 fine was known in Lancashire as the "sovereign remedy." Enforcement was a slow, painful process. The gradual education of public opinion to accept the need for regulation was not the least important part of it.

VII

TEN HOURS AND THE RELAY SYSTEM

After an important parliamentary select committee into the operation of the factory act, and many abortive bills, an amending act at length reached the statute book in 1844. This lowered the minimum age of employment to eight, but further reduced children's hours to $6\frac{1}{2}$ or 7, to be worked either before or after dinner. It forbade night work for women. It made some small but useful administrative changes, and plugged various loopholes in the 1833 act.

Three years later the Ten Hours act, covering young persons up to eighteen and all women, was at last passed. In the spring of 1848, Horner, after many doubts and much anxious enquiry among the workers, admitted that most operatives preferred more leisure, even at the cost of lower wages. By October he had come round to the Ten Hour men's argument that shorter hours were compensated by better work, and did not necessarily entail lower wages. The new act had been passed during a trade depression which decreased the demand for labour and so facilitated the observance of restrictions. But as trade revived the masters at last began to take seriously the relay system, which they realised could be made to stretch the ten hour working day for women and young persons to cover twelve hours or more for male adults. The amending act of 1844, foreseeing some such development, had laid down that the working day should be calculated from the time the first child or young person started work (except for children on the afternoon shift). Now schemes were introduced by which all started simultaneously, but different sets of women and adolescents had successive two hour gaps, their places being taken by a shift of adults. The adults' working day could now be extended indefinitely, the women and young people were kept hanging about all through it, and the Short Time committees found they had won a Pyrrhic victory. But now Horner took up the cause. He was determined that young workers should have their evenings free, to go to night school. He had to fight the masters, the justices, his own colleague James Stuart who supported relays, and a supine Home Secretary, Sir George Grey, who had to be forced to withdraw instructions against prosecuting for relay working. Cases were brought before Lancashire magistrates, but produced conflicting verdicts (one barrister J.P. actually went from session to session preventing convictions). A test case, *Ryder v. Mills*, was then brought in the court of exchequer. But the judges found that relays were not illegal under the act. The only remedy was further legislation. Ashley in parliament "betrayed" the symbol of Ten Hours and accepted the reality of an effective $10\frac{1}{2}$ hour day. He and Horner were now working on the same side. In 1850 an act forbidding relays was passed. This had to be amended when masters used the afternoon shift of children to prolong the day after the women and young persons had gone home. But by 1852 the legislative control of working hours for the young in cotton and worsted mills had become a reality, and the restriction of adult hours with it.

VIII

THE EXTENSION OF FACTORY CONTROL

In the early 1840's Inspector T. Jones Howell was lamenting that the education clauses had failed. His anglican colleague, R. J. Saunders, disagreed. He had hopes of building a real factory school system. Unwisely, as it turned out, Peel's Home Secretary, Sir James Graham, listened not only to Saunders' proposals for factory schools but to his plans for schools teaching religion from the church catechism, run by management committees chaired by the vicars, and inspected by the bishops. The resulting political row, led by dissenting millowners, defeated the scheme, and ruined any possibility of a state primary system growing from factory education.

After 1844 the inspectors turned with increased energy to the problem of factory safety. Stuart had long been campaigning for shields to protect wet flax spinners from hot spray. Now the inspectors exerted steadily increasing pressure for fencing dangerous machinery. Their reports publicised the disastrous accidents in which boys had their arms torn off, and women, caught by their hair in revolving shafts, were scalped. The safety regulations, gradually enacted, added to their enforcement duties.

When the inspectors saw children being taken by their parents from mills where their hours were restricted and sent to silk and lace factories, calico printing and rope-works, where, for a 10, 12 or 14 hour day they could earn a few extra shillings, they began to campaign for the extension of control. These trades were the last to be restricted, precisely because child labour was considered most essential to them. They now had an unfair advantage over the restricted manufacturers in attracting a scarce commodity. Lace factories where children were kept working in one position for three hours, and hanging about on the workshop floor all night, were exempt from the acts. Silk mills, which employed a high proportion of children to adults, had their labour limited to 10 hours under Althorp's act. Even after 1844 children in these mills became "young persons" at eleven.

In 1841 Ashley had procured a *Royal Commission on the Labour of Children in Mines and Colleries and other Unregulated Trades*. Tooke and Southwood Smith were again commissioners, with the two factory inspectors, Horner and Saunders. The commission's first report in 1842 contained sensational revelations of the coal industry: women and children, soaked to the skin, dragging heavy trucks through 18 inch underground passages, juvenile slavery, abuse by "butties" and miners, accidents, ill-health and immorality. The report was illustrated with prints which rapidly became famous. It had the intended effect, and an act of 1842 forbade the employment underground of women and girls and of boys under ten. The government appointed an 'Inspector of Mines', H. S. Tremenheere, and the law was partly enforced. But as the overriding need for safety regulations became apparent, together with the technical difficulties of inspection, the government became more unwilling to employ the necessary expert inspectors. The Home Office feared that responsibility for mine safety would be transferred from the mining companies to its own shoulders. Moreover, coal-owners, who were often large landowners, were entrenched in the inner circle of government in a way that middle-class cotton kings were not. Yet by 1852 a corps of mining experts was at work, and regulating acts accumulated throughout the century.

The commission's less sensational second report dealt with the hours of little 'teerers' in calico printing, a trade subject to the fluctuations of season and fashion. They proposed experimenting in compulsory education before the children went into employment, or during slack seasons. The enacted experiments were not a success; but they were at least a sign that the state's concern with the hours, conditions and education of working class children had become normal and was becoming universal.

IX

CONCLUSION

The industrial revolution which impelled parliament to intervene to protect the victims of technical advance, also brought Britain closer to class warfare than at any time since the Interregnum. Inevitably the administrators of the new laws became involved in the contemporary social stresses. Their tendency to give priority to the convenience of factory owners suggests that, to some extent, the inspectors were having to act against the grain of their own outlook and class prejudices. This, however, was mitigated by the fact that they were trying to control, not overturn, a system of which they approved. Few people criticised the employment of working class children in the "light and easy" labour of cotton mills so long as it did not damage their health or preclude "moral training". The children of the poorer classes always had worked as soon as they were capable of doing so, and nobody except the young John Stuart Mill (who was out of touch with working class life) or Robert Owen (who wished to keep them at school till twelve, but had to employ them at ten) suggested they should not. The controversy was not about labour, but about excessive labour and the education of children. The inspectors would have liked a national system of education. Meantime they were sensitive to the argument that too much restriction would cause children to be thrown out of work, when they would roam the streets since their parents would have no money for school fees. Yet the story of Stuart's methods in Scotland shows how easily protective laws could be made a means of oppression. Without men of open mind and moral stature such as Horner, the pioneer experiments in enforcement could have stoked the fires of class conflict.

Although they must have smarted from the attacks of the Short Time committees, most inspectors were sufficiently detached to hold some sort of balance between masters and men. They were ready to criticise a master for casting all the blame for law-breaking onto his workmen. They were equally ready to blame a parent for working his son, from the age of nine, twelve hours a day as a piecer, although, as Horner wrote bitterly, that same parent had probably petitioned parliament for protection of the poor factory children, "the white slaves" who were so cruelly overworked by "the hard-hearted, avaricious masters". If they were apt to defend the millowners they were confronting an avalanche of propaganda which did not distinguish too nicely between the law-abiding and the utterly unscrupulous. They were less conscious than the Short Time or trade union leaders of the economic compulsions which drove parents to sacrifice their children in the mills. At the same time, their charge that the Ten

Hour men were really indifferent to the welfare of the children was not completely answered. The 1833 commissioners' argument that a ten hour day would still leave small children too tired to be educated was incontrovertible, while Fielden's demand for an eight hour day for all was at that time economically and politically impracticable. On the other hand, a politically aware working class leader could have pointed out that Horner's view of the purpose of primary schooling was to check the feelings of alienation between employers and employed, so that "the just influence of property and education would be strengthened." A great gulf of experience and opinion lay between operatives and middle class inspectors. It was due to the bridge provided by the practical philanthropic tories such as Ashley that some cooperation was eventually established.

The history of the early factory acts may be related to a recent controversy about the causes and nature of the development in the nineteenth century of state intervention or social administration (what A. V. Dicey called "collectivism").[1] It offers evidence which supports the explanations offered by protagonists on both sides of the controversy. Here we see humane men finding the exploitation of children in factories and mines "intolerable", followed by the self-acting extension of public control arising out of practical administrative experience (the "model" presented by Oliver MacDonagh).[2] On the other hand we also see evidence of the deliberate influence on legislation and administrative methods exercised by the Benthamite group. Indeed, once Dicey's account, misleading in its definition of the aims of Benthamism, and superficial in its treatment of the factory legislation has been disposed of, the controversy seems somewhat artificial.[3] The analyses of the more recent historians do not conflict but complement each other.

This history also has a contemporary relevance all too easily forgotten. The factory acts provided a precedent for state action in a "free" economy to protect the weak, which made subsequent interventions that much easier. Yet every time technological

---

[1] A. V. Dicey, *Law and Public Opinion in England* (1905).

[2] O. G. M. MacDonagh, 'The nineteenth century revolution in government: a reappraisal', in *Historical Journal*, i (1958-9), an important contribution to the argument.

[3] Dicey saw the history of factory legislation purely in terms of a struggle between Ten Hour men and millowners and focussed on the Ten Hour act.

advance tempts the greedy, ignorant and indifferent to oppress the defenceless, destroy the common environment, and ruin the quality of life, all the problems which beset the first steps in social control revive. As the inspectors discovered, eternal vigilance is but a preliminary to the fight for social justice.

SELECT BIBLIOGRAPHY

Reports and evidence of select committees, royal commissions, the quarterly and the half-yearly reports of factory inspectors are scattered through the Parliamentary Papers. They have now been collected and republished in the Irish University Press edition of the *British Parliamentary Papers, Industrial Revolution, Children's Employment* Vols 1—15 (Vols 12—15 carry the reports on to 1876), and *Factories* Vols 1, 5—9.

Debate on Poulett Thomson's Factory Regulation Bill, *Hansard's Parliamentary Debates*, Third Series XXXIII (21 April—2 June, 1836) 737—788.

J. T. Ward, *The Factory Movement, 1830–1855* (1962), puts the Short Time movement in its place among other contemporary working class movements.

Cecil Driver, *Tory Radical* (1946), a life of Richard Oastler with an excellent detailed account of the Short Time movement and Northern tory-radical alliance.

J. C. Gill, *The Ten Hours Parson* (1959), a life of George Stringer Bull.

M. W. Thomas, *The Early Factory Legislation*. Thomas Bank Publishing Co. (Leigh on Sea) 1948, the essential account of the factory acts, the inspectors and the enforcement struggle. Useful appendix of documents.

A. H. Robson, *The Education of Children engaged in Industry in England, 1835–1876* (1931), an account of the acts emphasising educational clauses and administration.

S. E. Finer, *The Life and Times of Sir Edwin Chadwick* (1952). Chap. II, contains further lights on the royal commission of 1833 and the passing of Althorp's Act.

O. G. M. MacDonagh, "Coal Mines Regulation: The First Decade, 1842–1852," in *Ideas and Institutions of Victorian Britain*, ed. Robert Robson (1967).

John Fielden, *The Curse of the Factory System*. New edition with an introduction by J. T. Ward, Frank Cass 1969.

★ ★ ★ ★ ★

Related pamphlets published by the Historical Association include:

A15 W. H. Chaloner, *The Skilled Artisans during the Industrial Revolution* (1969)

G58 R. M. Hartwell, *The Industrial Revolution in England* (1965)

G61 F. C. Mather, *Chartism* (1965)

107 D. C. Somervell, *The Victorian Age* (2nd ed. 1969)